ABCs OF PERSONAL FULFILLMENT

A PRACTICAL GUIDE TO CULTIVATING RESILIENCE, JOY, AND PURPOSE

DR. ANGIE LESLIE

Copyright © 2024 Dr. Angie Leslie

All rights reserved. No part of this publication may be reproduced, distributed, or transmitted in any form or by any means, including photocopying, recording, or other electronic or mechanical methods, without the prior written permission of the publisher, except in the case of brief quotations embodied in critical reviews and certain other noncommercial uses permitted by copyright law.

Table of Contents

Author's Note

When Doves Fly

"Oh, I wish I had wings like a dove.
I would fly away and find a place to rest."
(NKJV Psalms 55:6)

Welcome to *ABCs of Personal Fulfillment: A Practical Guide to Cultivating Resilience, Joy, and Purpose*. Based on the book *"My Trauma is Not My Story,"* this companion workbook is designed as a roadmap for anyone seeking to discover and embrace their true purpose, cultivate resilience, and find joy in their everyday lives.

Purpose of this Book

The journey toward personal fulfillment is deeply personal and uniquely transformative. My aim with this workbook is to provide you with practical tools and spiritual insights to help you navigate your path to a more fulfilled and purposeful life. Drawing from my own experiences and faith, I share strategies to overcome trauma, embrace your true self, and align your life with your divine purpose. Through reflection, self-exploration, and faith-based practices, you will learn how to:

1. Recognize and Overcome Trauma: Understand the impact of past experiences on your current self and discover how to move beyond them.
2. Cultivate Resilience and Joy: Develop mental and emotional strength to handle life's challenges with a positive outlook.
3. Find and Fulfill Your Purpose: Align your daily actions with your core values and God's plan for your life to live a life of meaning and satisfaction.

How to Use this Book

ABCs of Personal Fulfillment is structured to guide you step-by-step through your journey. Here's how to get the most out of this workbook:

1. Reflect Deeply: Use the discussion questions at the end of each chapter to explore your own experiences and insights. These questions are designed to prompt deep reflection and personal growth.
2. Engage with the Content: Read each chapter thoughtfully and apply the principles to your life. The stories and insights shared are meant to inspire and guide you on your own path to fulfillment.
3. Apply Practical Strategies: Each chapter includes actionable steps and exercises. Implement these strategies to make tangible progress toward overcoming challenges and aligning with your purpose.

4. Connect with Your Faith: Throughout the workbook, you'll find spiritual reflections and biblical insights. Use these as a source of inspiration and strength, trusting that God's plan for you is unfolding with each step you take.

5. Build Your Personal Action Plan: At the end of the workbook, you'll create a personalized action plan to solidify your journey toward fulfillment. This plan will help you set meaningful goals, align your actions with your values, and stay committed to your growth.

Remember, the journey to personal fulfillment is ongoing and evolves with time. Approach this workbook with an open heart and mind, and let it be a companion in your quest for a life rich in resilience, joy, and purpose.

Thank you for allowing me to be part of your journey. May you find inspiration, growth, and fulfillment as you explore the pages ahead.

With warm regards,
Dr. Angie Leslie

Introduction

There Is Hope

God wants us to experience peace like the dove knowing that we are resting in His presence because we have dealt with every negative thought or opinion that we may have had about ourselves. What causes the most damage to our psyche is not what others think or feel; it is about what we think and feel about ourselves. When we are free from our own self-doubts, then we are also from others' opinions. Through the process of learning to fly, you will discover it's what God's thoughts are towards you that matters because He is the person orchestrating your future.

Synopsis

By embracing her identity, Adaeze learned that her worth is not defined by her past or by the opinions of others but by her own perception of herself and, ultimately, by God's view of her. Adaeze's story conveys resilience, showing that one's identity and life narrative can transcend past experiences. She emphasizes the importance of acknowledging trauma while also discovering the strength to overcome it. Through her journey, Adaeze inspires others to find their peace and purpose by trusting in God's guidance and seeing themselves through His loving perspective.

Using the guide below, briefly share your own trauma story:

Identify the Trauma: Start by thinking about the specific events or experiences that have been traumatic for you. What situations, people, or events do you consider traumatic in your life?

____

____

____

____

____

____

Acknowledge Emotional Impact: Consider how these traumatic events have made you feel. Have they caused feelings of fear, sadness, anger, confusion, or any other strong emotions?

____

____

____

____

____

____

Examine Behavioral Changes: Reflect on any changes in your behavior or habits since the trauma. Have you become more withdrawn, anxious, or aggressive? Are there new habits or patterns in your life that emerged because of the trauma?

____

____

____

____

____

____

____

Analyze Mental and Physical Health: Think about how the trauma has affected your mental and physical health. Have you experienced symptoms like anxiety, depression, insomnia, or physical health issues related to stress?

____

____

____

____

____

____

Look at Relationships: Consider how trauma has impacted your relationships with others. Has it caused trust issues, problems with communication, or difficulties in maintaining relationships?

____

____

____

____

____

____

Chapter One

He is Always There

Adaeze's personal journey illustrates the importance of addressing and healing from trauma as a crucial step in finding one's life's purpose. Her faith helped her realize that she was not taking this journey alone She learned that God had always been there with her just as He is with her now. This knowledge allowed her to actively work through past difficulties and shift her mindset towards resilience and positivity. Trusting in the Holy Spirit and to adjust her personal beliefs, provided the direction and support that she needed during those uncertain times. Adaeze also stresses that overcoming frustration and maintaining perseverance are essential for achieving one's dreams, even when confronted with significant challenges and limitations.

Overcoming Trauma and Pursuing Dreams Despite Limitations

- Adaeze discusses overcoming traumas to fulfill purpose and passion.
- Traumas can hinder dreams, but with God's help, trauma can be overcome.
- She reflects on feelings of emptiness and loneliness and the struggles of believing in herself despite the challenges of feeling invisible and mediocre. .

Role of Trauma and Struggle

How has past trauma or struggle impacted your perception of your purpose?

What steps have you taken, or can you take, to heal from the trauma to align your thoughts with God's view of you?

13

Chapter Two

There is a Plan

Adaeze's journey teaches us the importance of resilience and growth. Her journey allowed us to discover that true healing comes through self-discovery and empowerment. She learned that understanding one's calling and purpose is essential for a fulfilled life. Her path led her to the church, where she found healing and deliverance and a deeper understanding of God's plan for her life. Adaeze's story reminds us that no matter our past, God has a purpose for each of us, and by seeking Him, we can find the peace and strength to fulfill that purpose. Through church and spiritual growth, Adaeze discovered her identity and purpose.

Personal Growth and Ministry Building Through Love and Purpose

- Adaeze discovered her passion for teaching, researching, writing, and studying through her seminary education, which prepared her for ministry.
- Her journey of healing and love led to building ministries and a school, pouring into people, and mentoring.
- Building with love and purpose became the philosophy for Adaeze's future and destiny.

Finding Purpose and Building a New Life

- Adaeze discovers purpose in life through love and helping others.
- She reflects on her past experiences and realizes she has more to accomplish
- She realized that God's timing is perfect

Your Personal Connection to God's Plan

How do you interpret God's promise in Jeremiah 29:11 in your own life?

____

____

____

____

What plans do you believe that God has for you that have not been fulfilled yet?

Why have you not fulfilled them? What effect has your past had on you fulfilling God's plans for your life?

In what ways have you taken responsibility for positioning yourself to fulfill God's purpose for you?

What practical steps can you take to further align yourself with God's plan and purpose?

18

Chapter Three

Being made Whole

*"When Jesus saw him lying there and learned that he
had been in this condition for a long time, he asked him.
'Would thou be made whole?'" (John 5:6)*

Adaeze highlighted how her journey of recognizing and overcoming trauma profoundly impacted her ability to trust, love, and progress in life. She stressed that acknowledging and addressing trauma is crucial for achieving wholeness and freedom. Adaeze also shared her personal experience of faith in Jesus Christ, emphasizing that forgiveness is an essential step toward attaining true freedom and fulfillment.

The Act of Forgiveness and Its Impact on Life

- Adaeze acknowledges struggling with grief and low self-esteem and seeks to overcome them.
- She acknowledges childhood trauma impacting trust, love, and ability to move forward.
- She learned that despite the pain endured, in order to move forward she must forgive

Childhood Trauma, Deliverance, and Transformation

- Adaeze struggles with feeling free and whole due to unresolved childhood trauma.
- She describes a powerful deliverance experience by the Holy Spirit as the enemy was evicted.
- The Holy Spirit reminded the enemy that the house built by God belongs to Jesus, not the enemy, and it was time for eviction.
- Transformed from feeling empty and disconnected to experiencing peace and joy through deliverance and prayer.

Overcoming Past Trauma to Fulfill Ministry Calling

- Making room for my dreams to become a reality
- Acknowledgement is followed by action.
- Adaeze shares her journey of deliverance and healing from grief due to loss of normal childhood experiences.

Dreams and Desires

Despite challenges, what dreams and desires persist in your heart?

____

____

____

____

____

____

____

____

How do these dreams align with the understanding that God has a plan for your prosperity and hope?

____

____

____

____

____

____

Taking Responsibility for Purpose

Have you practiced the act of forgiveness?

____

____

____

____

____

____

22

____

____

If not, are you prepared to move forward by truly forgiving those who have hurt and/or disappointed you? If so, write down their names with the words "I forgive you" next to it.

____

____

____

____

____

____

____

Chapter Four

It's a Heart Thing

"For the Lord sees not as man sees; man looks on the outward appearance, but the Lord looks on the heart."
(1 Samuel 16:7b)

When it comes to implementation, God ensures that your heart is ready for it. Purpose is both a heart and mind thing. They both need to be synced with each other so that you will not easily give up when you are tested by the enemy. God will also test your willingness to see the assignment to the end. Only you know whether it's time to implement what the Lord has been revealing to you about yourself.

Overcoming Pain and Limitations to Reach Full Potential

- My plans will come to life, and my dreams will become a reality when I'm ready to live them.
- God wants us to reach for the stars and not settle for limitations.

- He wants us to deal with our pain points to live a fulfilling life.
- It is never too late to start pursuing one's dreams and desires with God's help.

Understanding Scripture and Applying Lessons

How do you study and apply the lessons from the Bible to your life, particularly in understanding your purpose?

____

____

____

____

____

____

Can you think of a biblical character whose story inspires you to pursue your purpose despite challenges? List the character and state why you are inspired by them and how you see their story playing out in your own life?

____

____

25

Chapter Five

See it to Completion

"Being confident of this very thing, that He who has begun a good work in you will carry it to completion until the day of Christ Jesus." (Philippians 1:6)

God divides up His plan for His kingdom and assigns each of us our portion of the building process. He introduces it to us slowly based on where we are in the acceptance process and our pursuit of growth. He keeps trusting us with more. Our natural limitations do not concern God because they are just temporary gaps. As we allow him to continue refining us, He closes those gaps throughout the transformation process until we become the vessel that we were intended to be at the point of our creation.

Feeling ready for the work involves these elements:

- Transformation
- Crossing over into contentment.
- The Importance of finding yourself

- Dealing with your pain points to live a fulfilling life.
- Knowing that it's never too late to start pursuing one's dreams and desires with God's help.
- The Lord provides resources needed

Overcoming the Enemy's Distractions

How do you recognize and combat feelings of insecurity, fear, and depression that might deflect you from your purpose?

____

____

____

____

____

____

What strategies can you implement to stay focused on God's plan for you?

____

____

____

28

Chapter Six

Romans Road to Transformation

"If you confess with your mouth the Lord and believe in your heart that God raised Him from the dead, you will be saved." (Romans 10:9)

After transforming her life, Adaeze now lives fully, appreciating the beauty and wonder of existence without the burdens of trauma. She expresses deep gratitude for her sense of purpose and the resources that have helped her achieve her goals. Adaeze shares how her relationship with God played a crucial role in her transformation, emphasizing the importance of aligning her mindset with God's will and the kingdom of heaven to lead a life of purpose and contentment.

Living Life to the Fullest With a Focus on Purpose and Ministry

- Adaeze feels energized and alive, living on purpose and excited about her assignment.

- She is focused on self-care and obedience.
- She reflects on her life journey, feeling fulfilled and content after sacrifices made for her family.
- Adaeze desires to help others realize their purpose and journey through writing and mentoring.

Spiritual Transformation and Growth

- Adaeze compares the transformative journey to 40 years in the wilderness, culminating in the rediscovery of identity and purpose.
- She encourages listeners to take the first step towards transformation, trusting in God's ability to make them whole.
- She expresses gratitude for God's transformation, acknowledging growth and alignment with His will.

Self-Examination and Belief in Worth

What areas of your life require deeper self-examination to understand why you might not be living in full purpose?

____

____

____

____

____

____

____

____

How can you build your belief in your worth and capability to live out God's plans for you?

____

____

____

____

____

____

Chapter Seven

You have been Chosen

"But you are a chosen people, a royal priesthood, a holy nation, God's special possession, that you may declare the praises of him who called you out of darkness into his wonderful light." (1 Peter 2:9)

God has chosen you to live a life of purpose and meaning, which involves changing your narrative to reflect your identity in Him, living intentionally according to His will, manifesting your dreams with faith and surrender, and trusting in His provision as you work towards a vision for the future.

Changing Your Narrative

Taking control of your personal narrative means recognizing that you are not defined by your past or by others' opinions but by the identity and purpose God has given you. To reflect your true self, you must align your thoughts and actions with God's truth about who you are. Consider the changes you can make in your daily life to better tell the story of who you are in

God's eyes. This might mean letting go of negative self-talk, embracing the gifts God has given you, and living out your faith boldly. By making these changes, you can ensure that your life reflects the beauty and purpose that God sees in you.

Living on Purpose

Living "on purpose" means being intentional in every aspect of your life, making choices that align with God's will and your divine calling. It involves setting clear goals that reflect your faith and values and taking actions that move you closer to fulfilling your God-given purpose. To ensure that your actions and decisions reflect this, seek God's guidance in prayer, stay grounded in His Word, and surround yourself with people who encourage and support your spiritual journey. When you face setbacks and frustrations, remember that these are opportunities for growth. Trust in God's plan, learn from your experiences, and remain steadfast in your faith, knowing that He is with you every step of the way.

Manifestation of Dreams

The process of manifestation is about partnering with God to bring your dreams and purpose to life. It begins with believing in the promises God has for you and actively taking steps toward those promises. If there are areas where you feel stuck, remember that these are not permanent obstacles but rather opportunities for growth and deeper faith. To progressively work towards the manifestation of your dreams and purpose, spend time in prayer, seeking God's guidance and clarity. Take small, consistent steps each day that align with your goals, and trust that God is directing your path. Surround yourself with positive influences and keep your focus on God's vision for your life, knowing that He will bring your dreams to fruition in His perfect timing.

Trusting in God's Provision

Trusting that God will provide the necessary resources for your purpose means believing that He knows your needs even before you do. It requires faith that God's timing is perfect and that He will supply everything you need to fulfill your calling, whether that's financial support, the right people, or other resources. Reflect on moments when God has come through for you unexpectedly, showing His faithfulness and provision. For example, think of a time when you were in need, and God provided in a way you never anticipated, like a financial breakthrough, a supportive friend, or a new opportunity that opened doors. These experiences remind us that God is always at work, orchestrating everything for our good and His glory.

Faith and Surrender

Faith plays a crucial role in your ability to surrender to God's plans, as it gives you the confidence to trust that His ways are higher than yours. When you believe that God is good and has a purpose for your life, it becomes easier to let go of your own plans and submit to His will, even when you don't fully understand it. To maintain a mindset of trust and surrender, engage in practices like daily prayer and meditation on Scripture, which keep you connected to God's presence. Regularly remind yourself of God's past faithfulness and how He has guided you before. Surround yourself with a community of believers who encourage and support your spiritual journey. By doing these things, you can cultivate a heart that is open to God's leading and a mind that is at peace with His timing.

Vision for the Future

Your vision for the future should align with God's plans for you, reflecting His purpose and direction for your life. It involves understanding the unique path He has set out for you and how you can contribute to His greater plan. To move closer to that vision, start by setting clear, actionable goals that reflect your faith and aspirations. Break these goals into smaller, manageable steps and take practical actions each day that bring you closer to achieving them. Seek God's guidance through prayer, and be open to His adjustments along the way. Surround yourself with supportive individuals who share your values and can offer encouragement. By consistently aligning your daily actions with your vision, you demonstrate your commitment to following God's plan and trusting in His provision.

Your Personal Fulfillment

Now, it's time to explore the profound journey of aligning your thoughts to achieve personal fulfillment and growth.

We'll begin by defining what personal fulfillment truly means and examine the characteristics of individuals who actively pursue it. Understanding what it takes to achieve this state, including overcoming challenges and fears, is crucial for anyone looking to fulfill their potential.

We'll discuss the essential elements required for personal fulfillment, the key to reaching it, and the importance of creating a fulfillment-focused identity. This exploration will lay the groundwork for building a better version of yourself, emphasizing personal growth, self-awareness, and the alignment of actions with core values and beliefs.

By creating and implementing a strategic action plan, you will be empowered to connect your daily actions with your deeper values and goals, ultimately leading to a life of purpose and satisfaction.

Are You Ready?

Aligning My Thoughts

1. What is personal fulfillment?

____

____

____

____

____

2. What are the characteristics of individuals who pursue personal fulfillment?

____

____

____

____

____

3. What is required to achieve personal fulfillment?

____

____

____

____

____

4. What are the challenges people face that make them afraid
    to pursue fulfillment?

____

____

____

____

____

5. What is the key to achieving personal fulfillment?

____

____

____

____

____

6. How and why do we need to create a fulfillment-focused identity?

____

____

____

____

____

Building A Better Me

A. Recognizing the Call to Personal Growth

- Understand that personal growth is a lifelong journey and begins with a desire to improve oneself, supported by a mind ready to embrace change and new possibilities.

B. Exploring Identity and Purpose

- Delve into who you are and what you are meant to do. Reflect on your passions, talents, and values to uncover your purpose, ensuring your mind is clear and focused.

C. Cultivating Self-Awareness

- Become more aware of your thoughts, emotions, and behaviors. Self-awareness is the foundation of personal growth and mental clarity.

D. Tools and Techniques for Self-Exploration

- Utilize methods such as journaling, meditation, personality assessments, and feedback from others to deepen your understanding of yourself and prepare your mind for growth.

How are you preparing your mind for growth?

Cultivating My Purpose

A. Aligning with Core Values and Beliefs: ABCs of Personal Fulfillment

- Clarify what truly matters to you. Your core values will guide your decisions and actions, and your mental clarity will ensure you stay aligned with them.

B. Building a Solid Foundation: Connecting Actions with Personal Values

- Ensure that your daily actions reflect your values. This connection, supported by a sound mind, leads to greater satisfaction and fulfillment.

C. Creating and Implementing Meaningful Goals and Objectives

- Set goals that are meaningful and align with your purpose. A clear mind is essential for setting and achieving these goals.
- Develop a plan that summarizes the steps you will take to achieve your goals and live according to your values with mental clarity guiding your journey.

My Plan of Action

Describe the steps that you are planning to take to start creating your own fulfullment plan?

About the Author

 Dr. Angie Leslie is the founder and CEO of Antioch-Global, a private non-profit Christian organization focused on discipleship training and leadership development as well as the founder and CEO of Dr. Angie Leslie Ministries and Spark Academy. The latter two of which is the basis for this work. She love helping people achieve their goals and succeed in life. Success looks differently for everyone, and Dr. Angie's call is to assist those assigned to me with defining what success looks like for them.

Achieving success means letting go of past hurts and failures to focus on your future. Having been a child of emotional abuse, she know what it's like to feel lost, helpless, and alone. Experiencing any level of trauma is devasting to a person's ability to move forward because you are constantly reminded of the pain but with God's help all things are possible. Dr. Angie's role as a mentor is to create a safe place for people, mainly women, to be able to share and support each other as we all work to heal together. Through group mentoring sessions, we will learn to celebrate our wins and comfort each other through our losses.

Contact information

Please be sure to check out our blog at sparkacademy.com, where we celebrate each other's wins and comfort each other during times of loss.

Visit us at DALM.com for other books by the author, including ***My Trauma is Not My Story,*** and for more details regarding our monthly group mentorship program: My Thoughts Matter

You can also purchase the guidebook ***My Thoughts Matter*** to get on the road to having a sound Mind.

www.ingramcontent.com/pod-product-compliance
Lightning Source LLC
Chambersburg PA
CBHW040113150726
48005CB00013B/1691